Sacagawea

Indian Interpreter to Lewis and Clark

by Marion Marsh Brown

 CHILDRENS PRESS®
CHICAGO

PICTURE ACKNOWLEDGMENTS

State Historical Society, North Dakota Heritage Center—Frontispiece
Denver Public Library—page 12
Historical Pictures Service, Chicago—pages 20, 36, 52, 74, 76, 82, 112
Reproduced from the collection of the Library of Congress—pages 68, 88
Oregon Department of Transportation—page 69
North Wind Picture Archives—pages 70 (2 photos), 72, 73, 75 (2 photos)
Montana Historical Society, Helena—page 71
Cover illustration by Len W. Meents

CURR
F
592.7
.S123
B76
1988

Library of Congress Cataloging in Publication Data

Brown, Marion Marsh.
  Sacagawea: Indian interpreter to Lewis and Clark.

  Includes index.
  Summary: Relates the story of the young Shoshoni Indian woman who acted as a guide and interpreter for the Lewis and Clark expedition.
  1. Sacagawea, 1786-1884—Juvenile literature. 2. Lewis and Clark Expedition (1804-1806)—Juvenile literature. 3. Shoshoni Indians—Biography—Juvenile literature. 4. Translators—United States—Biography—Juvenile literature. [1. Sacagawea, 1786-1884. 2. Shoshoni Indians—Biography. 3. Indians of North America—Biography. 4. Lewis and Clark Expedition (1804-1806)] I. Title.
  F592.7.S123B76 1988 973'.0497 [B][92] 87-33810
  ISBN 0-516-03262-3

FOREWORD

I am pleased to be the consultant for this work. It is unique in that it is a junior-level story about Sacagawea that is based on documented history. The journals of Lewis and Clark make it possible to walk history's rigid line with accuracy. Long lost in a maze of myth and half-truths, the gentle young Shoshone of the Lewis and Clark Expedition emerges here as a true American heroine. Furthermore, the story is charmingly told by Marion Marsh Brown without the use of invented superwoman feats.

An early book, based on assumptions made before key documents surfaced, gave Sacagawea a wrong identity and spelled her name "Sacajawea." To clarify the name: "Sacagawea" is used sixteen times in the journals and is described as a Hidatsa word meaning *bird woman.*

Diarists who knew Sacagawea after the journey ended described her as "good . . . of a mild and gentle disposition . . . the best woman in the fort . . . and greatly attached to the whites."

After the journey, Clark kept in touch with Sacagawea. St. Louis archives reveal that, faithful friend to the last, Clark became legal guardian of motherless Baptiste (Pomp) and his baby sister, Lisette, in 1813. Some years later, Clark made an entry in his ledger—now deposited in Chicago's Newberry Library—establishing Sacagawea's early death.

Pomp was educated in St. Louis and Europe, where he mingled with royalty. But this did not alter his love for the frontier, to which he returned. He was a highly respected, polished, intellectual mountain man. He died on May 16, 1866 at Inskip Station in southeastern Oregon.

Credit must be given to Irving Anderson of the Lewis and Clark Trail Heritage Foundation, Inc. for tirelessly unraveling fact from fiction in determining what happened to Sacagawea and Pomp after the captains closed their worn field books.

Blanche Schroer

Table of Contents

Chapter 1

CAPTURE!

It was a lovely sunny summer's day, and two young Indian girls were enjoying it as much as were the birds and the little animals of the forest. They darted here and there to pick wild strawberries, laughing as they popped the sweet red fruit into their mouths and wiped the juice from their chins with quick brown hands.

"He-toe! He-toe!" one of the girls called to the other, pointing out another patch of berries she had discovered.

Her friend smiled. She liked being called He-toe, for the word sounded like the call of a bird she loved. Her friend said she called her by this bird name because she reminded her of a bird, always so quick, flitting here and there. Well,

He-toe thought, a little giggle gurgling in her throat, she would like to be a bird. She would like to be able to fly far, far into the distance and see what the rest of the world was like.

She was always happy when her tribe went on a buffalo hunt, for then she saw new and different things. But she had no idea that one day she would go much farther than her people had ever gone, and see countless new sights, more than she had ever dreamed of seeing.

The two girls were of the Lemhi Shoshone tribe, who lived on the western slopes of the mountains. All of the tribe, except the old women and the very small children, had come to this wide valley that spread out from a big muddy river, on a buffalo hunt.

To the girls, a buffalo hunt was like a wonderful, extended picnic. To the men, the hunt was an exciting challenge and very important, for on its success depended not only their winter's supply of meat but also hides for their clothing. To the women, the hunt meant much hard work, for after the animals were killed, it was their job to cut up the meat and prepare it for drying, then to scrape and tan the hides, and eventually to make from them all of their wearing apparel, from moccasins to robes. Not quite old enough to be required to work with the women, the girls were carefree and happy, with no thought of lurking danger.

The Shoshones had almost no guns, but they had horses,

which many other tribes did not have but coveted. The Shoshones had acquired their horses through trade with the Spaniards who had come seeking gold, and they were very proud of their mounts. Cameahwait, an older brother of the girl her friends called He-toe, came galloping by where the girls were sitting on a grassy bank. He shouted that he was joining the men who were forming a semicircle around the buffalo herd to push the animals over the cliff. It had been the decision of the council to use this method for the kill rather than the slower, more difficult method of shooting the buffalo with bows and arrows. Besides being easier, it also would yield more meat.

He-toe listened. Yes, she could hear the bellowing of the beasts. "Ooh! Tonight we will have a great feast," she cried, in Shoshone. She hugged her flat belly and rocked back and forth in delighted anticipation. Food had been scarce in recent weeks. Meat from the last buffalo hunt had long been gone, and the small game the hunters brought in from day to day had not provided enough food to keep the pangs of hunger away.

He-toe had a great curiosity concerning the world around her, and now as she sat listening to the roar of the buffalo, like distant thunder, she was wondering what the animals that were not killed would do. Would they run, with their lumbering gait, back to some safe place they called home, as her people did when enemy tribes threatened them? Would they follow this river that so intrigued her? Where did the river go?

But suddenly her dreamy, wondering mood vanished. Her ear had caught a different sound, and now she concentrated all her senses on that sound—on what it meant and from where it had come. It was nearby! She did not cry out to her friend. She had been schooled since babyhood against making an outcry in the face of danger. Her body tensed like a bowstring and her eyes sought those of her friend, questioning. Yes, she had heard it too! In absolute quiet, they waited. Then from behind them came a sudden shrill cry of stark terror. The women! From the place where the women had been waiting for the men to return with the kill came shriek after shriek, punctuated by gutteral shouts of triumph.

Now the girls knew. They had been attacked!

He-toe leaped to her feet, at the same instant darting a quick look behind her. What she saw horrified her and filled her heart with terror. Strange men, painted with ugly yellow stripes, were wielding clubs and tomahawks among the screaming women. Still without making a sound, she slid down the bank into the swirling waters of the river and began to swim downstream with the current. If only they wouldn't see her! Just a few yards ahead she could see a snag of driftwood hugging the shore and she felt a surge of hope. It could be a hideaway! If she could only reach it! When she was younger she had sometimes dived under such a shelter

16

when hiding from her playmates. If she could just get under this one! She was directly opposite it now. She dived, hoping the water was deep enough. But all hope died at that very instant, for a strong arm had grabbed her shoulders and held her in a vise. Then something came down hard on her head and all was blackness.

When she came to, she was among strangers, around a campfire. It was evening. After she had blinked her eyes a couple of times, she cast a quick glance about to see if there were others of her people among the strangers. Yes! She spied two girls of her tribe, one of them her very own friend with whom she had been eating strawberries when the enemy struck. But there was no way she could reach the girls, for she was bound with leather thongs.

After a little she struggled to sit up and an old woman, seeing that she was conscious, brought her a bowl of food. It smelled delicious and was steaming hot. It must have just then been taken from the big kettle that hung over the fire. The captive girl's black eyes spoke their thanks to the squaw, and when her arms were loosed, she ate hungrily. Then the thought came to her that she was eating meat from the buffalo her people had killed. *And how many people were killed?* she wondered. Her mother, certainly, for part of the horror that had met her eyes before she fled was an attack on her mother, which would surely have resulted in death.

The next morning before the sun was up, there began

what was to be a long trek eastward. The girl whom her friend had called He-toe the day before no longer moved like a bird. She trudged among the women, who, seeing that she did not try to escape, loosened her bonds.

Now she felt freer and began observing with interest the country through which they were passing. There were different grasses, different wildflowers, even, after a time, different bird songs. All of this greatly interested her. But there were no mountains! Would she never again see mountains, towering peaks that had cradled her in security since birth? While this thought saddened her, her mind very soon turned to the present and she was wondering what lay ahead.

One night after the camp was asleep, her friend crept close and whispered that she and the other Shoshone girl were going to try to escape that very night, before they got so far away that they might never find their way home. Would she come with them?

A chance to get back to her people! But what if the runaways should be captured again? Wouldn't things go hard for them then? Or if they did succeed in getting back to their mountain home, what then? Would there be any food? No buffalo meat, certainly. She remembered the hunger pangs she had suffered. She was being well fed here! And would there be any of her family left?

She did not sleep. Around and around in her head churned

her thoughts. When at last the camp was completely still and the night was black, she watched two figures stealthily rise and come toward her. As they passed, her friend touched her shoulder. But she did not move. She had made up her mind.

Building winter quarters for the Lewis and Clark expedition

Chapter 2

A NEW NAME

When the long trek was over, the one lone remaining Shoshone captive found much to interest her in the Hidatsa village to which she had been taken. The life-style of the Hidatsas was very different from that of her people. First of all, the village did not look at all like the one she was used to because the homes here were not made of skins like those of the Shoshones. She was curious about them because they did not look as if they could easily be taken down and moved from place to place as could those of her people. As the months went by, she was to discover the reason for this: The Hidatsas were not a nomadic people. This village was their permanent home.

Another thing that amazed her was that instead of just going out and digging roots and picking berries for food, the Hidatsas dug holes with sticks and planted seeds that grew into strange plants from which they harvested and stored food for the winter months: maize and squash and beans. She, the captive girl, was very soon put to work helping to take care of these crops.

This was a new life, and to go with that life she was given a Hidatsa name, Sa-ca-ga-we-a. All of this seemed strange to her at first, strange, but exciting. Her childhood was over. No longer could she spend her days playing as she had at home.

Now, as a slave, she must work side by side with the women of this tribe. Most of the time she was treated well enough, but sometimes she was beaten, and at times like these she wished she had run away with the other Shoshone girls. But she hadn't. This was her life now, and there was much that she liked about it; first of all there was always plenty to eat. The busy days grew quickly into weeks, the weeks into months, and the months into years.

Two white men lived with the Indians in this village, both French-Canadians, one named Jussome, the other Charbonneau. One day the squaw who was in charge of Sacagawea told her that the white man named Charbonneau wanted her for his wife and that she was to move into his hut. Charbonneau was much older than Sacagawea, and he already had one wife, also a Shoshone. He was following the ways of the Indians, and this included not only having more than one wife, but also treating squaws as inferiors whose place in life was to work, to feed the men, wait on them, and bear their children. So Sacagawea took up these duties around the fire of Charbonneau.

After a time she found that she was pregnant, and she was glad. She liked the idea of having a papoose to care for and to love. Although she had seen only sixteen summers and was small of stature, she felt herself to be a woman, ready for the responsibilities of motherhood.

One late afternoon in the fall, when Sacagawea was large with child, there was great excitement in the village. It began with a big boom that frightened Sacagawea, for surely it was the sound of "the fire stick," which had been much feared by her people. But the Hidatsas were not running away in fright. They were running toward the river in the direction from which the noise had come. Quickly Sacagawea followed. She must know what all the excitement was about. As she approached the shore, she saw that several canoes and two larger boats, one red and one white, were being anchored, and that the men in the boats were white, except for one who, wonder of wonders, was black.

These men seemed to be saying that they were friends, for they dangled brightly colored beads from their fingers and held them out toward the Indians. But if they were friends,

Sacagawea wondered, why had they shot off the fire stick? She hurried to find Charbonneau. He would know.

Though usually impatient with Sacagawea's questions, Charbonneau this time seemed glad enough to answer them. He was important now, for he could understand what was being said and so knew what this exciting happening was all about.

The big boom? That was just to let the Indians know the boats were coming, he said. These men had traveled a long way on the river, he continued to explain to Sacagawea, but it was their plan to go much farther, clear to the Big Water. The men in charge, who were now coming ashore, were Captain Meriwether Lewis and Captain William Clark.

Why did one of the captains have that strange red hair? Sacagawea wanted to know.

There were many white men who had red hair, Charbonneau answered. And some had hair the color of the yellow squash she had tended. It just grew that way.

So many new things, strange and exciting, she was learning! But the black man? Had he painted himself all over with burned wood?

No! Charbonneau said with a sardonic laugh. *He just grew that way*, with black skin.

This was almost more than Sacagawea could believe. That there were white men with red and squash-colored hair was amazing enough. But black skin?

These men had come from St. Louis, Charbonneau went on. They were on their way West to try to find a passage over the mountains in order to reach the Big Water. But as it was nearing the time of the big cold when snow would fall and the river would freeze over, they wished to winter here and wait until spring to continue their journey.

"To live with *us*?" Sacagawea wanted to know.

"Don't be a goose," Charbonneau said loftily. "They will build their own winter quarters."

They were looking for a good place, perhaps a little farther down the river, but they wanted the Hidatsas to know they were friendly, that they had brought them gifts, and that they would like to smoke the peace pipe with them tomorrow.

But why did they want to go all that way? Was it just to see the Big Water? (That would be reason enough, she thought. She could not even imagine what the Big Water would be like. Like the sky, perhaps?)

Sacagawea's last question Charbonneau found more difficult to answer than the others. After a moment's hesitation he said it was because the Great White Father in Washington wished it. He wanted the captains to blaze a trail that white men from the East could follow to reach the Big Water. Perhaps to trade.

Sacagawea was beside herself with excitement. She continued to hurl questions at Charbonneau as they stood watching the men debark. What a brave, adventurous thing these men were doing, she thought. The distance was long between here and the mountains. And to go *over* the mountains? That would require much courage and much stamina. And what good would canoes and pirogues be when the men reached the mountains? She threw that question at Charbonneau, but he only shook his head. He was thinking of something else now and had no more time for her questions. He was going to go see the captains, perhaps as early as tomorrow. He had just had an idea—an idea that would bring something more amazing to Sacagawea than she could have dreamed of.

Chapter 3

AMAZING OPPORTUNITY

A few days later, when the sound of hammer and saw rang through the woods, telling the Indians that the white men were building their winter shelters, Charbonneau announced that he was going to pay the captains a visit. Sacagawea, ever curious, asked to go along. What kind of shelters were these white men building? And even more, what were the men like? Those curious men—the redheaded one? The black one? She wished very much to see them again.

At first Charbonneau denied her request, but finally he grudgingly agreed, and they set out, Sacagawea trailing respectfully behind her husband, as was the Indian custom.

As they approached the area where trees had been felled and huts were already going up, Sacagawea's heartbeat quickened. So much activity! So much noise! Shouting and laughter! It was not at all like what she was used to, with the women quietly doing all the work, while the men sat and smoked or mounted their horses and disappeared. Curious as a kitten, her eyes bright with interest, she took in everything: the heavy sticks with shiny heads that must be very sharp for they took quick bites out of sturdy trees when men swung them at the trunks; the way the logs were being fitted together as the huts went up; the scuttling about of the men; the strange, heavy boots they wore on their feet. But where was the black man? The redheaded one?

Soon, following Charbonneau, she saw the redhead, for he was one of those Charbonneau had come to see, and whom he had now found and, with the help of an interpreter, was engaging in conversation. Sacagawea did wish that she could understand what they were saying, but she had not learned the French language, which her husband was now speaking. He was directing his words to a Frenchman who could speak English, and who, in turn, was translating them into English for the captains.

Suddenly, however, her attention was caught by a word one of the captains spoke, the word "Shoshone," the name of her own tribe! Why? It seemed to her that the men's discussion went on interminably, but at last they seemed to have finished, for there was much nodding of heads, and then each captain in turn shook Charbonneau's hand.

"What is it? What were you talking about? Why did they say 'Shoshone'?" she demanded of Charbonneau the minute he turned from the captains and they started toward home.

"I was asking them to take me along as interpreter when they go on their long journey."

"You are going away—with them?" Sacagawea asked in astonishment.

Charbonneau nodded his head. "You too," he said gruffly.

"Me?" This was totally unbelievable, beyond Sacagawea's ability to comprehend.

"Why?"

"Because you're Shoshone."

But Sacagawea just shook her head. She didn't understand this at all.

"Why—why should I go because I'm Shoshone?" she asked in bewilderment.

"Because they will go through the country of your people, and you can speak for them there. They will need horses to go over the mountains. They have heard that the Shoshones have horses."

Now Sacagawea was beginning to make a little sense of it all. "They want *me* to help them get horses from my people?"

Charbonneau nodded. "To interpret, when they reach Shoshone country."

29

This was almost too big a thought for her. She was going to get to see her people again? She was going along with these strange men as they made their long journey? Suddenly she thought of her baby who would be born in a few months.

"The papoose?" she demanded of Charbonneau.

Again he nodded.

She and her baby and Charbonneau were all to go? The idea loomed as large as the mountains whose shadows had cradled her, an adventure beyond imagining. To see her people again! To show them that she had a husband and child! This much she *could* imagine. She would concentrate on this part of the tremendous future that had suddenly been spread before her, too large, too strange, too new for her to comprehend.

Chapter 4

POMP, "FIRST BORN"

As the weeks went by, however, and Sacagawea frequently visited the white men's camp with Charbonneau,
she came to accept and believe in this wonderful thing that
was going to happen in her life: that she was going to
accompany the captains and the other white men and her
husband on a long trek that would not only take her back to
her homeland but also across the towering peaks of the
mountains in whose shadows she lived as a child. Then on,
even to the Big Water, of which she had heard but which she
had never dreamed of seeing. It sounded like going to the
end of the world, and to Sacagawea, who loved seeing new
things, it beckoned enticingly. Her heart those days was

high with hope and her head was full of dreams.

To the possibilities of hardships and dangers on the journey she never gave a thought.

Then came the day when Charbonneau told her they had been invited to spend the next months with the white men in their winter quarters. They were to live in one of the log cabins! This was most amazing to Sacagawea.

"But why?" she asked her husband. "Why do they want us to live with them?"

Charbonneau shrugged. "To get used to how they do things, maybe, so we'll be more help on the trail. I don't know."

By the first of February, when it was nearing the time for Sacagawea's baby to be born, she felt quite at home in the white men's quarters. Her Hidatsa friends came there frequently for medical help. The captains had a goodly supply of medicines and were generous with them. Almost daily a squaw would come with a sick child to be treated, or a brave with a wound that was festering. Often it was someone whom Sacagawea knew well, and she would visit with the "patient" as he was treated, watching with bright eyes, eager to learn the white men's skills.

Sacagawea helped wherever she could in the camp, learning what the men liked best to eat and how to cook it to please them. The rest of her time she spent making soft clothing of skin for her baby, and more moccasins for Charbonneau and herself, for she well knew their moccasins would soon wear out on the long trail they were to set out on in the spring.

She had learned much about the group in the weeks she had been with them: Charbonneau had been right about the black man. The black did not wash off. She had watched the man splash water on his face and scrub his hands with soap, and when he dried she observed that there was no black on the towel. She had learned too that he was jolly. She liked him. He was called York.

The man who put a strange gourd-shaped thing with strings across it on his shoulder and then hit these strings with a stick he called a "bow" was a fascination to her. Sometimes when he drew his bow across the strings, the other men did a funny dance that made Sacagawea laugh. "They look like grasshoppers, the way they jump up and down," she told Charbonneau.

"They're dancing a jig," Charbonneau told her.

Certainly this jig was nothing like an Indian dance, and the "music" produced on the stringed thing that they called a "fiddle" was nothing like that of the Indians' drums. The man who played the fiddle was called Cruzatte.

Of the two captains, Sacagawea liked Captain Clark much the better because he was so friendly. He (of the red hair) had started calling her "Janie." She didn't know why he called her that, but she liked the way he said the name, for he made it sound as if he liked *her*. When he called, "Janie," she came quickly, to help him with whatever chore it was in which he needed assistance.

The other captain, Captain Lewis, spent a lot of time writing in a big book, and he was the "Medicine Man." It was he who got out the medical supplies when someone came for help. Sacagawea felt great respect for him, even though she did not enjoy his company as she did that of Captain Clark.

It was a cold winter, that winter of 1804-1805, the ground covered deep in snow. Sacagawea didn't mind the cold, however. When she went walking under the stars on a black night or on a bright night when the moon was full, her heart sang. Yet when it was time for her baby to be born, she was glad of the warmth of the log cabin.

Charbonneau sent for the old women of the tribe who were good at helping in childbirth, for Sacagawea's baby did not want to come easily. The old women used all their skill; Captain Lewis got out his medicines; but still they could not relieve Sacagawea's pain nor hasten the birth. As the long hours dragged on, everyone was concerned for Sacagawea's life. Finally, the Frenchman, Jussome, said he had heard that the dried rattles from a rattlesnake, given to a woman in labor, were helpful. Captain Lewis had some rattles among the things he was collecting to take back to President Thomas Jefferson. He got them out and crumbled "two rings" into small bits, mashed them in water, and handed them to a squaw to give Sacagawea. Dutifully, she drank the concoction and ten minutes later her baby was born!

There was great relief and rejoicing in the camp. Sacagawea held her baby happily and proudly displayed him for the white men to admire.

"He's a fine boy!" Charbonneau bragged. "See? Perfect! I name him Jean Baptiste."

Sacagawea knew that Charbonneau was naming their son for his friend Jean Baptiste Trudeau, another Frenchman who had spent time at the Hidatsa village. This was all right with her, but she knew she would not call the baby Jean. She would call him Pomp, which in the language of the Shoshone meant "First Born."

It was on February the eleventh that Pomp was born, and he soon became the pet of the camp. The men were happy to have a baby in their midst. It broke the monotony of the long winter days. With the temperature hovering at 10 degrees below zero, it would be a while before they would start watching for the winter snows to melt and the river ice to break up. They didn't feel so isolated from their homes with a mother and child living with them. So the months now were very pleasant for Sacagawea. She felt one of the group; she was happy to have her baby admired; and there was the wonderful adventure that lay ahead, when spring should come.

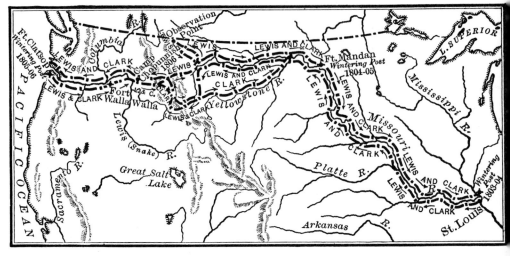

A map showing the route taken by Lewis and Clark

Chapter 5

START OF THE LONG TREK WEST

The first sign of spring came to Sacagawea one night when she heard wild geese trumpeting. *"They're going north,"* she said to herself. *"They know that the moons of snow are leaving and the moons of green leaves are coming."* It was a sound she had always loved, but this year it meant more to her than ever before. Her heart sang.

A few weeks later when she heard the ice in the river grinding as it began to thaw and break up, she knew that the time of departure was drawing near. The men of course knew too, and activity in the winter quarters of Captains Lewis and Clark increased tenfold. The men packed and repacked, trying to make loads lighter; trying to get their supplies they would need from day to day in boxes that would be easily accessible. Then, when the sun was melting the snow into small rivulets of water that cut their way to join the river, they began working on the boats.

By the first of April, all was in readiness. They had planned to load the boats that day, but a hailstorm kept them inside the cabins. Although Sacagawea was eager to get started, she took this delay more calmly than the men, who were annoyed and impatient. In her sixteen years she had learned to take things as they came, and the foibles of the weather were just something to be accepted.

Three days later the weather had cleared, and on a bright, sunshiny day Sacagawea helped load boxes onto the barge. Little did she realize at the time the importance of their contents. In these boxes were the tools for collecting scientific materials from the vast West into which the expedition would be venturing—materials later to be delivered to the Great White Father.

In the next two days they loaded the red and the white pirogues. Everything was in readiness by the night of April 6. Sacagawea slept little that night. Although she did not show her excitement, her heart and her thoughts were racing. She wakened very early on the morning of April 7 and was up before the sun. Little Pomp was fed and cared for and strapped on her back on a cradle board by the time the men were stirring. There was much hustle and excitement then as the final items were stowed in the canoes.

As the dawn streaked the sky, many Hidatsas started arriving at the landing, come to see the party off. Sacagawea was proud to have them see her stepping into the canoe that had been designated for her, her baby serenely sleeping on her back. No longer was she a captive slave! The white men wanted her on their expedition and this was a very big thing. She could see that the Indians on the shore recognized this; they showed their approval by their friendly good-byes.

As the captains shouted orders and the caravan of two pirogues and six canoes started up the river, Sacagawea for a moment stood tall in the canoe and lifted her hand in farewell. A great surge of happiness washed over her. The too-strange-to-believe future that had opened before her on the day Charbonneau had told her the captains wished her to accompany them had become the present. They were off!

The boats made good time. The river was smooth and caused them no problems. Sacagawea thought this was surely the happiest day of her life; except, perhaps, for the day Pomp was born.

After a time Captain Clark hailed Charbonneau and asked if he and Sacagawea were getting tired of their cramped positions in the canoe. Would they like to walk with him for a while? Sacagawea was glad for the change. She walked lightly in her moccasins, easily keeping up with the long strides of the men and eagerly taking in the sights and sounds of spring on shore. Many of the wildflowers and plants she recognized. Some of the plants she knew were "good medicine." Some were sources of food. But there were things, too, that were new to her, and these she wished she could stop and examine. Oh, the world was full of so many interesting things, and now that her life was expanding she would get to see more of them than she had ever dreamed.

By the time the sun was sinking low and the shadows of the trees on shore began to lengthen, Sacagawea was again in the canoe, and word went from boat to boat that the captains were looking for a good place to spend the night, and that as soon as they found a satisfactory spot they would be tying up the boats and making camp. It was not long until such a spot was found.

As the necessities for the night were unloaded, Captain Lewis was checking his book. "The way I figure it, we made more than twenty-five miles today."

"Very good!" said Captain Clark. "At this rate we should have no difficulty in getting over the mountains before the snows come."

Sacagawea couldn't understand what they were saying, but she could understand that they were pleased. Certainly, *she* was pleased. What a beautiful day it had been! And she had been observing something along the shore that she wanted to investigate.

As some of the men went out with their guns to secure

game for the evening meal and others built a campfire and made preparations for the night, Sacagawea went off by herself. She found a pointed stick and then walked along, slowly, with her eyes on the ground. She had seen a number of mounds of dirt that said "gophers" to her, and now she was looking for some of these "gopher holes" near the campsite. When she found one, she dug in with her sharp stick and brought out some small oval-shaped tubers that she collected happily. She found several more gopher holes and went back to camp with a good supply of the vegetables they yielded.

"What are they?" the men wanted to know when she returned and proudly exhibited them.

She asked Charbonneau to tell them that they were good eating, that she would cook them for supper. They were wild artichokes, she said. The gophers dug them and stored them in their holes. They too thought them good eating!

She laid Pomp on a fur blanket. "You are only a little more than two moons old," she said to him, "and look what an adventure you are having." She set about cleaning the vegetables as the good smell of wild turkey roasting on a spit over the bonfire filled the air.

Later, as they sat about the campfire eating, Captain Clark praised Sacagawea for her contribution to the meal. "Good! They're very good!" he exclaimed beaming. The other men chimed in, in agreement.

"It is much better for us that we have vegetables as well as meat in our diet," Captain Lewis said.

When Sacagawea lay down for the night, with little Pomp beside her, and the big sky sprinkled with stars overhead, she felt utter contentment; she was at one with the world about her. The men had praised her on their very first day out. Surely this was a good omen.

Chapter 6

SUPPLIES OVERBOARD!

The spring days continued to be pleasant as the procession of boats moved steadily westward. The caravan passed what the captains said was the mouth of the Little Missouri. Near this point Sacagawea pointed out wild geese nesting in the trees. The men agreed with her that the goose eggs would be good eating. They would surely try to rob a nest that evening. But a little later as she caught sight of a mother goose hastily leading her fuzzy little goslings into the protection of the forest, Sacagawea laughed. She guessed they were a little late for goose eggs!

As the days went by, the grassy plains were left behind and stretches of sagebrush took their place. The water became alkali.

"Tell the men not to drink the water," Sacagawea said to Charbonneau one evening when they had made camp. "It might make them sick." Charbonneau reported, and Sacagawea was pleased to see the captains nodding their heads.

The next day they came to the mouth of a big river that seemed to excite the men very much. That night Charbonneau told Sacagawea that Englishmen, who had been there earlier, named the river the "Yellowstone."

"But," cried Sacagawea, "the Hidatsas say that long, long ago the *Indians* named it that because of the color of the canyon walls!"

One sunny afternoon a few days later, when everything had been going well and the river was causing no problems, Charbonneau was given the responsibility of manning the white pirogue. Riding with him were Sacagawea and little Pomp, Cruzatte the fiddler, and a couple more of the men. Charbonneau was taking it easy at the helm, for the day had been calm throughout. But all of a sudden a squall came up, and without warning, it slapped the pirogue, hard, whirling it around and leveling the sail to the water. The boat tipped on its side, and all was pandemonium.

Charbonneau, who could not swim, panicked. "Help! Help!" he cried. The men on shore shouted advice, but Charbonneau was too frightened to hear or heed it. Cruzatte sprang to his aid, working madly to right the boat. Sacagawea saw boxes of supplies tip overboard and go bobbing about in the river. She watched with consternation, seeing a box she knew contained tools, a box of food and supplies, and worst of all—the medicine chest—wash overboard.

Those precious supplies must not be lost! From the rear of the pirogue, she leaned perilously over the edge, grabbed the nearest box, and threw it back into the boat. But others were out of her reach, bobbing on the waves and getting farther and farther away. She grabbed a paddle, kept in the pirogue for use at times when the wind stilled, and reached out with it, persistently pulling box after box within her reach. As she pulled in the last box, she saw that the men had succeeded in righting the craft and were hastily bailing out the water that it had taken on. Though water-soaked, the supplies had been saved, and Sacagawea smiled to herself. It had been quite an adventure, something to break the monotony that sometimes overcame the expedition on days when nothing happened.

That evening at the campsite as Sacagawea was helping to unpack the soggy supplies and spread them near the fire to dry, Captain Clark gave her a pat on the back and said, "Good work, Janie! I doubt we would ever have gotten these necessaries back if it hadn't been for you. You have a good head on you and you're a brave one."

Although Sacagawea was beginning to understand some of the strange words the white men used, she did not know all of those that went with Redhead's smile and pat on the back. However, she was well aware that she was being praised. This made her feel special, for neither the Hidatsa nor the Shoshone squaws were used to praise. Her heart sang at the very wonderful turn her life had taken.

Chapter 7

ILLNESS STRIKES SACAGAWEA

June came on and the weather turned hot, but frequent thunder storms cooled the travelers and were thus welcome. Most days now Sacagawea was among the walkers. She could see more when walking and besides she preferred it to the inactivity of sitting long hours in a canoe or pirogue. The men commented on how strong she was. Charbonneau told her that the captains even wrote this about her in their journals. He told her this scornfully, showing his anger, for he, like the Indians among whom he had long lived, did not believe in a squaw's receiving praise or attention. Sacagawea herself simply thought it strange that the captains should write about her at all in their books. She was just a squaw of no importance and was only along because neither Charbonneau nor Jussome could speak Shoshone. One evening they camped where others had obviously camped before them. There were the blackened remains of a campfire, and the sagebrush surrounding it had been trampled flat.

"Indians!" exclaimed Captain Lewis. He was pleased. They had been traveling now for a month, making good headway. Perhaps they were nearing the homeland of the Shoshones. He called Sacagawea and Charbonneau to him, and asked if Sacagawea recognized this place. Were they nearing her people's villages? But Sacagawea shook her head.

"But perhaps some of your people camped here, out on a hunt?" he asked.

Sacagawea did not answer this immediately. Instead, she examined the footprints about the campfire. Then again she shook her head. No, they were not Shoshone who had camped here. "Assiniboins," she announced.

But how could she tell? Captain Lewis wanted to know.

Charbonneau pointed to the footprints, but shrugged; maybe those; he didn't know.

Sacagawea was still examining the ground. When she made her report to the captains, it was complete, and they shook their heads in wonder. Not only did she tell them what tribe had camped here; she also told how many were in the party. "Not just men," she said, "but women and children."

She also reported how long the Indians had stayed at this place, and how recently they had left it.

Sacagawea was happy. She had pleased the captains again. She had felt especially rewarded by the warmth in Redhead's voice when he had said, "Good work, Janie!"

By the beginning of June, the party had come to where the river forked. They were not sure which branch to follow. After scouting both branches for several days, the captains decided their first hunch had been right. It was the south branch that was the Missouri and that they must follow.

One day when Sacagawea was walking as usual, a rainstorm drenched the party, and then a sharp, chill wind came up. Whether or not this was the cause, Sacagawea developed a bad cold. For a couple of days she kept up her usual pace, but then she began feeling really miserable, with cramps in her abdomen. The men insisted that she ride in one of the pirogues. She lay down in the bottom of the boat, which was so unusual for her that her companions were alarmed. A boiling sun was beating down on the boats, and Captain Clark suggested that they move Sacagawea to the rear of the pirogue where a canvas covering gave some shade.

"She's so hot," he said, touching her forehead. Sacagawea opened her eyes and moaned softly as they moved her. "There. Maybe that will be better," Clark said.

When Sacagawea heard his voice, she looked up and said, "Pomp."

"Yes, Janie, we'll take care of Pomp," he assured her.

"She has a fever," he said to Charbonneau. "We'll have to see what some of our medicines will do for her when we make camp tonight and can get to them."

When they stopped for the night, Captain Lewis looked at Sacagawea and shook his head. "She's very sick," he said. He went to the medicine box and looked over its contents. "I just don't know," he said to Captain Clark, "what to treat her for. It seemed to start with that cold she caught." Finally he got out some tablets and mashed two of them in a spoonful of water. He carried the spoon to where Sacagawea was lying. "Hold her head up," he said to Charbonneau. But Sacagawea pursed her lips and turned her head aside when they approached.

Charbonneau spoke roughly to her. "You do what the Captain says! He's trying to make you better."

But still she refused to take the medicine.

Captain Clark joined them. "Come on, Janie," he begged gently. "Be a good girl. We need you."

"See?" Charbonneau translated. "He says they need you." Then he added with a sneer. "Don't forget why they brought you along."

This argument worked and she opened her mouth for the medicine. But she did not smile, and her usually bright eyes were dull.

Although she continued, reluctantly, to take the medicine,

it was not effective and the captains became more and more worried. They continued on their way, with Sacagawea lying listless in the back of the pirogue. She would not eat, and often she doubled her knees up in pain.

"She's just wasting away before our eyes," Captain Lewis fretted. Although he didn't say so, he was concerned for their expedition as well as for Sacagawea and her baby. What would happen if she were not able to translate for them when they reached the land of the Shoshones?

A couple of nights later they camped not far from a mineral spring. Captain Clark had an idea. He filled a mug with the cold water in the spring and took it to Sacagawea. She drank it thirstily, as if knowing that it was what she needed.

The captains conferred that night and decided to remain at this campsite for a few days, allowing Sacagawea to rest undisturbed, and to continue giving her water from the mineral spring.

By the end of the next day she was showing signs of improvement, and everyone was much relieved. Another day and she was speaking to them, "Sa'i!" she said, which they had learned was her word for "good." By the third day she was up and caring for Pomp, and her eyes were bright again.

On the fourth day they started on their way, and Sacagawea seemed completely recovered. That day's journeying was very gay.

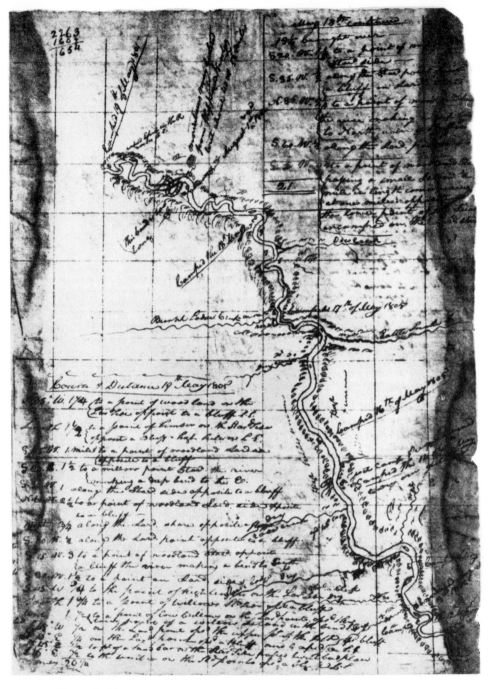

William Clark's map and notes covering a section of the Missouri River

Chapter 8

A WALL OF WATER

According to the captains' computations, it was now the middle of June. Hot, sultry days made the difficult river travel almost unbearable. The men's dispositions were becoming prickly. It was time for a break in the daily routine that had been slowly, desperately pushing the expedition westward.

A decision was made when an inviting cottonwood grove appeared on shore. They would camp here. They set about building carts to carry the boats and supplies when the possibility of further river travel should run out. They knew such a time was coming, though how soon they did not know.

Finally the day came when they were to set out again.

They would still struggle on the river with the boats, but much of the baggage went into the carts. Sacagawea chose to walk with the men who were pulling and pushing the carts. She was excited, knowing that every day they proceeded would surely bring her nearer to her people. She tried to do her share in helping to pull the carts, but the men, except for Charbonneau, were reluctant to accept her help in this heavy task.

Before the first day of walking and pulling the cumbersome carts was over, they came upon prickly pear cactus, and no matter how they tried to avoid it, they were soon tramping on the plants, which promptly stuck their sharp spines through the soles of everyone's moccasins. Sacagawea suffered with the men, and at night when they made camp, sat pulling the needles from her feet. She was glad Pomp wasn't big enough to walk!

When Captain Clark finally finished pulling the spines from his feet, he threw his arms in the air and shouted, "Seventeen!" Then, seeing that Sacagawea was puzzled by his outburst, he pointed to his feet, then held up his fingers: two hands, one hand, and two more fingers, to show her how many needles he had removed.

Sacagawea had to laugh. White men were very funny, counting things.

One afternoon when Captain Clark, Charbonneau, and Sacagawea, with Pomp on her back, were walking, a violent storm came up. Sheets of rain came down with such force that they could scarcely stand, nor could they see their way. So Captain Clark pushed the others under a rock ledge that extended out from the bank of a creek they had been following. Then with a sharp ejaculation of relief, he followed to the shelter, shaking water from his hair and eyes.

They had not been in their newly found shelter five minutes, however, when they saw a mammoth wall of water coming toward them.

Charbonneau gave a sharp cry of fear and scrambled as fast as he could up the slippery bank.

"Pull her up!" Clark yelled, pushing Sacagawea to the bank.

Charbonneau reached for her hand and pulled. But the bank was very slick, and the pelting rain blinded her. She seemed to fall back faster than he could pull her up. Suddenly Captain Clark shoved her upward, and she managed to get one knee over the ledge. Charbonneau pulled harder and she had made it.

She looked down and saw to her horror that Captain Clark stood in water up to his waist. But in an instant, as soon as he saw Sacagawea and Pomp were out of danger, he pulled himself up, hand over hand, to safety.

The little group sat huddled in the drenching rain, seeing below them, in the very spot where they had stood minutes before, a great wall of water crashing.

"It's at least fifteen feet deep down there now," Clark said. "That was a mighty close call."

Their close call had been precipitated by what the captain called a cloudburst, and its fury lasted only minutes. When it subsided, Sacagawea, cradling Pomp in her arms, said her word of appreciation, "Sa'i!"

By the time all members of the party were reunited, the rain had turned to hail, which pelted them piteously. They decided to camp for the night on a little island in the river. One of the men came proudly bearing into camp his prize: "The biggest hailstone ever seen by man!" The others crowded around, and soon someone brought out what Sacagawea had come to know as their "measuring stick."

"Seven inches around!" its finder cried.

Counting and measuring things. They're so funny, Sacagawea thought again.

Cruzatte took his fiddle from its wet case. Carefully he examined the instrument. "I think it survived," he said, beaming. He struck up a tentative chord. "Yup! No damage done. We'll tune her up after supper and celebrate everybody's safety and the biggest hailstone ever."

Sacagawea sat by the fire drying her own clothing and her baby's. She hoped Cruzatte would play a jig. That would be the kind of music that would express how she felt tonight.

Chapter 9

"HER PEOPLE"

Mountains! At long last, their pale blue outlines appeared on the horizon, barely discernible against the blue of the sky. The Lewis and Clark party had been looking for them for so long that it was almost like a dream when they were finally sighted. Sacagawea was the only one of the group who had ever seen these mountains before. They meant home to her. Though she did not indicate it to her companions, she was very excited by the realization that they must be getting close to the land of the Shoshones, her people!

The same day that they sighted the mountains, they came to a creek that Sacagawea recognized, and now her excitement ran high. With eyes shining, she looked up from the bank where she had scooped up a handful of mud, and chattered excitedly, holding the mud out for the others to see. Charbonneau translated what she was saying: "This is a creek where my people came for the white clay to use for paint!" The spirits of the captains and the men rose to match Sacagawea's exuberance. There were smiles and laughter and jokes to lighten that day's load.

The next evening when the captains were looking for a good camping place for the night, Sacagawea's attention was focused on every feature of the landscape. As they trudged along, she looked to right and left: This was familiar territory. Suddenly she stopped, spreading her arms and pointing. This was the very spot where her people had been camped that fateful day five years ago when she was kidnapped by the Hidatsas!

Knowing from Sacagawea's account that they must now be getting close to the Shoshones' homeland, the captains decided to make camp on the spot.

Sacagawea ran from place to place explaining to Charbonneau that here was the place where she and her friend were eating wild strawberries when they were set upon. Here was where she jumped into the river, hoping to be able to hide under some driftwood. And finally, she pointed to the middle of the river, saying that here she was captured. Charbonneau translated her story to the white men.

The jovial mood of the travelers continued. Surely now

they would meet the Shoshones very soon. The Shoshones from whom they must get horses for crossing those mountains that had been looming more distinctly every day. It was almost the end of July.

But another week went by, and they had seen no Indians. Sacagawea was beginning to be concerned. Where were her people? However, a day came when she recognized a high point on the plain they were crossing and told the men that this was not far from the place where her tribe spent their summers. Now they would find the Lemhi Shoshones soon. She was in territory that she knew. But as days went by, she became more and more troubled.

But Sacagawea's concern about the whereabouts of her people was overshadowed by another concern. Captain Clark, having injured his ankle, was suffering from infection. Despite the wild-onion poultices that she applied and the medicines that Captain Lewis gave him, it was becoming increasingly difficult for him to walk. To leave the river and go into the mountains in search of the Shoshones had become out of the question for the redheaded one.

Late one night, after a lengthy conference among the men, Charbonneau explained to Sacagawea that they had decided Captain Lewis should take a small body of men with him and go on the search alone while Captain Clark should remain in charge of the main body of men on the river. It was already the first of August, and the captains were desperate to find the Shoshones, get horses from them, and get over the mountains before the snows came.

"We are not to go with Captain Lewis?" Sacagawea asked Charbonneau in dismay.

Charbonneau shook his head. "We go on up the river with Captain Clark."

At first Sacagawea was greatly disappointed by this. If Captain Lewis found her people, she wanted to be there at the meeting. And hadn't the captains brought her along to interpret the Shoshone language?

But then she thought of poor Captain Clark. He needed her. It was best that she remain to take care of his infected ankle. The infection was spreading throughout his body, and she was very worried about him.

So the next morning, torn two ways, Sacagawea watched the little party set out in search of her people.

Time now dragged interminably, as the main party with Clark continued to toil up the river. Days went by, and no word came from Captain Lewis. Sacagawea could see that the redhead was worried, but at least she thought his ankle looked a little less ugly. One evening he shook his head and said sadly, "They've been gone a week. Is it possible that we will never see them again?"

After being told what he had said, Sacagawea shook her head violently and stomped her foot. "We *will* see them, I tell you. We *will* see them—and my people."

But another day went by with no sight of the searchers or the Shoshones. Then on the morning of the 17th of August, when navigating the Missouri was becoming almost impossible, though some of the men were still struggling to push the boats over the rocks in the river, Sacagawea's faith was rewarded.

It was still early morning, so the air was fresh and cool, and she was reveling in the chance to walk. She was also feeling happy because Captain Clark's ankle was better. In fact, he too was walking. She ran on ahead of him and Charbonneau, feeling the joy of the morning.

Suddenly she stopped. Then, as suddenly, she began to run and to cry out. But her cries were cries of happiness, for she had seen advancing toward her a troop of men, women, and children who were her people, Lemhi Shoshones!

For just an instant she stopped and turned back to those behind her. Jumping up and down in delight, she put the fingers of her right hand in her mouth and sucked on them.

"Her tribe," Charbonneau explained to Captain Clark. "It means 'We are of the same blood.' She is telling us that they are her people, the Lemhi Shoshone."

Her eyes misted with tears, Sacagawea searched eagerly for faces she knew in the approaching group. Then suddenly a young woman broke from the ranks and ran to Sacagawea. She threw her arms around her, and the two held each other in a joyously tearful embrace. It was the friend of her childhood, the friend with whom she had been picking strawberries when the Hidatsas attacked, the friend who had been captured with her but who had escaped. She *had* made it back home!

Chapter 10

DRAMATIC MEETING

The minutes became hours. There was so much for each of the young women to tell the other. And the old women, friends of Sacagawea's mother, gathered around, wanting to hear her story, wanting to see Pomp, whom she displayed with great pride.

Suddenly she heard her name called in Charbonneau's angry voice. He was coming toward the group of which she was the center, beckoning and shouting: "What are you doing? Get over here! The captains want you! This instant!"

The captains? Then Captain Lewis must have found the Shoshones. She had been so excited she hadn't even seen him. She had seen only her people.

"They want you to interpret," Charbonneau said. "What are you along for? What's the matter with you? Hurry! They want you *now!*"

He led her to where the men, Indians and whites, sat in a circle on the ground. She saw instantly that they had been smoking a peace pipe. This was good! Her people and her friends. She saw too that all present had removed their moccasins, a sign of goodwill. Quickly she stepped out of her small ones, then seated herself at the outer edge of the circle, and bowed her head. Squaws were not ordinarily allowed at such a meeting; this was most unusual and she felt humble. She wondered if the chief were with this group, and who was the chief of the Lemhi Shoshones now. Her father had held that position when she was with the tribe. So many thoughts tumbled through her mind! So many emotions tore at her heart.

An Indian voice began to speak. The chief? She raised her head. This was a voice she knew!

With a little half sob of a cry, she jumped to her feet and ran to the chief. She threw her blanket around him, crying glad tears. It was her brother Cameahwait! The brother whom she had last seen on the day of her capture five years before, riding his horse proudly, going to take part in the buffalo kill!

Charbonneau explained to the captains what was happening: that the chief was Sacagawea's brother; that the act of enfolding them both in her blanket was the sign that they were of the same parentage.

Sacagawea, through her tears of joy, asked about the other members of her family. All gone, Cameahwait said sadly, all except their one brother, who was back at the village, and the little son of their sister. Sacagawea's tears flowed harder, but at last she tore herself away and returned to her place. The tears would not cease, but through them she managed to interpret to her brother and the other chieftains assembled that these white men were friends, that they were going across the mountains, and that they needed horses for the trip. They were asking to trade with the Lemhi Shoshone tribe for some of their horses.

The conference over, Sacagawea was free to rejoin her friends. As she ran about trying to explain her presence and the fact that she was not to remain with the tribe, it became obvious to her that her people were in a state of near starvation. As she knew that game had been very scarce during the recent days on the trail, she understood their predicament.

There was little that she could do to help them, for the white men's supplies were low. But she remembered a "sugar loaf" she had not eaten when it was given to her one day as part of her rations. She had saved the little cube of sweetness for Pomp. But now she went to her leather pouch and took it out. She found Cameahwait and gave it to him, telling him to eat, and explaining that it was very good. Cameahwait instantly put the sugar cube in his mouth. He was ecstatic over the taste. Never had he tasted anything so good, he said.

Sacagawea knew that hunters had been sent out by the white men. But would they come back empty-handed? As evening came on, she had her answer. The hunters returned, but they had among them only one deer. Sacagawea was instructed to go with the hunter who carried it, to take the animal to the chief, and to tell him that the white men wished to make him a gift of it.

Before long, as she ate flour-and-water cakes with the men of the expedition, she could smell the aroma of meat cooking. Her people were cooking the deer, not on a spit over an open fire as the white men would have done, but boiling it in a big kettle. This way it would go farther, and Sacagawea knew that the broth would be used to give the children some nourishment. She was glad. She had found her sister's little son and had been saddened by his thin little body. He was such a contrast to Pomp, who at seven months was plump and healthy. She would see that her nephew got some of the broth from the deer tonight, and perhaps the hunters would do better tomorrow.

They did. They brought in two deer and an antelope. This time the captains' party came in for a share, but Sacagawea saved most of her portion, to make sure her small nephew and the family caring for him would have enough to eat that night. She was not happy about the condition in which she found her tribe. She had done the right thing, she believed, staying with the Hidatsas. Their living conditions were much better than those of the Shoshone, and in their location they were less beset by enemy tribes. Besides, had she not been with the Hidatsas, she would not have had Pomp. Nor would she have been on this wondrous adventure that had already been so rewarding and that was still to lead her to the Big Water.

Even though Sacagawea believed her main job—introducing the captains and their party to the Shoshone and explaining their need for horses—was over, still Charbonneau had been hired for the whole trip, and she was to go with him. She looked forward to crossing the mountains, and even more to seeing the Big Water, which intrigued her because they were beyond her imagination.

But a very important job still lay ahead for her, with the Lemhi Shoshone, a job of which she as yet knew nothing, and it would be vital to the expedition.

Lewis and Clark holding a meeting with Indians

A diorama showing the Lewis and Clark party at Celilo Falls, Oregon, on their way to the Pacific Ocean

Meriwether Lewis

William Clark

York, the black member of the expedition

Grouse
are
about
short
and eye.
Cock
Cock
which
on the
and
hood
Mountains
to the Mountain
the Columbia
the great falls
they go in large
or singularly

the feathers about its head
pointed and stiff. Some hairs
the base of the beak. feathers
fine and stiff about the ears.
This is a faint likeness of the
of the Plains or Heath
the first of those fowls
we met with was
Missouri below
in the neighbour=
of the Rocky
and from
which pass,
between
and Rapids
Gorges
and
make

hide hide remarkably close when pursued,
short flights &c
The Large Black & White Pheasant is peculiar
to that portion of the Rocky Mountains watered by
the Columbia River. at least we did not see them while
we reached the waters of that river, nor since we have
left those mountains. they are about the size of a
well grown hen. the contour of the bird is much
that of the redish brown Pheasant common to
our country. the tail is proportionably as long and is
composed of 18 feathers of equal length. of a uniform
dark brown tiped with black. the feathers of the
body are of a dark brown black and white. the black

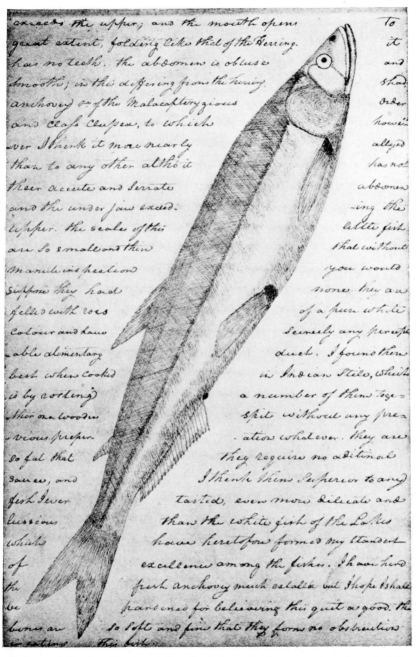

exceeds the upper; and the mouth opens to
great extent, folding like that of the Herring. it
has no teeth. the abdomen is obtuse and
smooth; in this differing from the herring, shad
anchovey or of the Malacaptory gious order
and class Clupea, to which howe-
-ver I think it more nearly alleyed
than to any other altho' it has no
their accute and serrate abdomen
and the under jaw exceed- -ing the
upper. the scales of this little fish
are so small and thin that without
manute inspection you would
suppose they had none they are
felled with roes of a pure white
colour and have scercely any percepti-
able alimentary duct. I found them
best when cooked in Indian Stile, which
is by roasting a number of them toge=
ther on a wooden spit without any pre=
vious prepar- -ation whatever. they are
so fat that they require no aditional
sauce, and I think them superior to any
flesh I ever tasted. even more dilicate and
luscious than the white fish of the Lakes
which have heretofore formed my standard
of excellence among the fishes. I have herd
the fresh anchovey much extalld but I hope I shall
be pardoned for believing this quit as good. the
bones are so soft and fine that they form no obstruction
in eating this fish.

Clark carefully described and sketched the animals encountered west of the Mississippi River.

our rout lay along the ridge of a high mountain course S 20. W. 18. me used the snow for cooking. –

Thursday September 19th 1805.

Set out this morning a little after sunrise an continued our rout about the same course of yesterday or S. 20. W. for 6 miles when the ridge terminated and we to our inexpressable joy discovered a large tract of Prairie country lying to the S. W. and widining as it appeared to extend to the W. through that plain the Indian informed us that the columbia river, (in which we were in surch) run. this plain appeared to be about 60 Miles distant, but our guide assured us that we should reach its borders tomorro the appearance of this country, our only hope for subsistance greatly, revived the sperits of the party already reduced and much weakend for the want of food. – the country is thickly covired with a very

An entry in the diary of Meriwether Lewis for Thursday, September 19, 1805

The Columbia River (above) and the mountains (below)

Sacagawea was overjoyed to find her Shoshone people.

Chapter 11

NEAR DISASTER

Charbonneau was not as popular with the men of the expedition as was Sacagawea. He did not have her even disposition or her willingness to take orders. He was often surly. But Sacagawea obeyed him and took his abuse because she had been brought up in a culture that believed that a squaw was chattel and as such could be handled by her husband as he willed.

While the expedition party was in the Lemhi Shoshone camp, Sacagawea, despite Charbonneau's unpleasant disposition and sometime harsh treatment, had reason to be glad that he was her husband. A young brave in the tribe went to her brother Cameahwait and demanded her in marriage, saying that her father had promised her to him a long time ago. He had given her father a fine horse as his part of the bargain. Cameahwait called Sacagawea to him, but when she appeared with Charbonneau, her husband, and Pomp, her son, the Shoshone who would have claimed her said that it was too late, and the incident was closed.

Sacagawea was grateful. She wanted to go on with the captains, to finish the journey with them. She realized too that she would no longer wish to live among her people who were often hungry, never secure in the future. Life with the Hidatsas and life with the white men was much better. She would be sad to leave her brother and her little nephew and her friends, but her life now must go on in the direction it had taken.

The expedition party was laying plans to start off soon. Sacagawea had negotiated for twenty horses from the Shoshone. One, a very good pony, had been designated for her to ride. Also guides had been secured to go with them, an older man called Toby, with long experience in the mountains, and his four sons.

Then one morning when Sacagawea was playing with her small nephew and her baby, Charbonneau called her name angrily. He was in an ugly mood, for he had just been chastised by the captains for not telling them sooner of something he had learned several days before: that the Lemhi Shoshone were planning to leave very shortly on a buffalo hunt, taking all their horses, including those they had promised the captains, as well as the guides that had been hired. The expedition could not possibly be delayed for the time a buffalo hunt would take. They needed to start very soon in order to get across the mountains before winter storms would make crossing impossible.

All of this Charbonneau poured out to Sacagawea in a torrent of angry words as he jerked her up by the hair, and pushed her ahead of him. "The captains want you. *Now*," he ended.

Sacagawea soon learned why the captains wanted her. They needed her to interpret for them as they put their predicament before the chief and his subchiefs and tried to dissuade the tribe from their plans. First she went to Cameahwait, but he turned her away, saying that the tribe was starving and they must get meat. Also they had told another Indian tribe that they would meet them at a certain time and place for this hunt, for the greater safety of numbers should an enemy tribe attack. So they needed to go at this time.

Sacagawea pleaded that the white men must have the horses and the guides *now* or their expedition would never make it over the mountains. In Shoshone, she said to him, "You gave your word. The Lemhi Shoshone do not go back on their promises." Still, he insisted the hunt was more important.

Finally Captain Lewis told her to ask her brother to call a council meeting so they could put their case before those men who represented the tribe. Cameahwait nodded his head to this and Sacagawea felt some relief. When the council was convened, she was again called in to interpret. The session was long. Discouraged as the afternoon wore on, Sacagawea translated over and over the pleas of the captains. Into Shoshone she put their words: "We dare not delay!" Time and again she repeated what she thought was their strongest argument: "We trusted you." Captain Lewis said, "We were told the Shoshone were a people of their word." And he reminded them of the goods they had already received in payment for the horses.

All of this Sacagawea translated, and then she put in her own plea: "It is true," she said, "what they say. I have often told them I am proud of my people because of their sense of honor."

She had almost given up when suddenly she heard a different tone in the murmurings about her. What were they saying? She listened intently. *It was true that they were a people of their word. Perhaps the whole tribe need not go on the hunt. Perhaps just the best hunters.*

Hopefully Sacagawea looked at Cameahwait, and he nodded his head.

Success at last! Her eyes alight, she turned to the captains to give them the good news. Once again she had come through for them. Once again she had been of great value to the expedition. She was happy.

It had been a long day for her, but when Captain Clark asked her to bargain for another ten horses, she went about the task willingly. It was not an easy task, for the tribesmen wanted guns as barter, and these the white men did not have beyond those needed for survival.

Finally after a better offer from the captains, including two guns, she was successful in getting nine more mounts, so that they totaled twenty-nine when they prepared to depart the next day.

Sacagawea, with little Pomp strapped on her back, rode proudly as they left her people. Her sadness at leaving was offset by the knowledge that she had done her job well and by the anticipation of new adventures ahead.

Meriwether Lewis looking at the Rockies the expedition had to cross

Chapter 12

DANGEROUS PASSAGE

On their first day out of the Shoshone's camp, Sacagawea noticed that the sunflower heads were bending toward the earth, brown now and heavy with seeds. This was joy to her, a fine start for their journey, for when they stopped for the night she would gather of this harvest. Mashed into meal, the sunflower seeds made fine eating. Such meal had long been a favorite food of the Shoshone; she remembered it well from her childhood. She knew that the party's supply of flour was low, and they had been warned by her people that once they reached the mountains, game would be very sparse. Hence scarcity of food would be a problem.

In the next few days she was very glad she had gathered

the sunflower seed when she did, for as they drew nearer the mountains, the temperature dropped so much that there was ice in the early morning in their water utensils. It was good to be able to make a hot porridge for breakfast.

On the last day of August they left their campsite at sunrise. When they found a grassy area along a creek, they stopped for several hours to let their horses graze, for they were coming into the foothills very soon, and their mounts needed sustenance. They could see prairie fires in several directions, which Sacagawea explained were signal fires among different Indian tribes, all of whom were probably assembling for the big buffalo hunt in which her people were to participate.

The next morning as they started northwest across the hills, riding became difficult. Not only were the hills steep and rocky, but also they were covered with thickets of brush and scrubby trees. Time and again the men had to cut away the underbrush before they could proceed. At these times, Sacagawea would dismount and go berry hunting. Running from patch to patch of fat ripe berries, she would gather enough so that each man would have a handful for his lunch or dinner. When she returned to the group after one such forage, she learned that the four sons of Toby had disappeared. Sacagawea was not surprised; they probably had gone to join the Lemhi Shoshones who by now would be on their way to meet the other tribes who were going for buffalo. Now there would be four fewer mouths to feed from the captains' meager supplies. It was as well that they had gone.

As the expedition struggled on, it began to rain, making the rocky hillside slick and treacherous. Guiding her mount carefully, thinking not so much of her own safety as that of little Pomp, Sacagawea was following the trail slowly when suddenly the line of riders ahead of her halted. She could not see what had happened. Perhaps they had come to another thicket that must be cleared. Soon, however, Charbonneau, who had been riding ahead, came back in great excitement with the news that a horse had slipped and fallen, injuring itself. The men were now removing the baggage from its back. There would be some considerable delay as it would take a while for them to find how badly the horse was hurt and what to do with it. Probably, Charbonneau said, it would have to be shot.

A short time later a shot rang out. Sacagawea shuddered.

Soon the line moved on, slowly, with horses continually slipping on the wet rocks that bore them steeply upward. This was the Lolo trail, old Toby had told Sacagawea, who translated his Shoshone words to Charbonneau in Hidatsa. "Very old, very treacherous," but it would take them over the Bitterroot Mountains the best way, the only way he knew. So if they were to reach the rivers that would take them west to the Big Water, they must make this crossing.

That night the hunters brought in only two pheasants for the evening meal.

The next morning when they wakened, they found the rain had turned to snow and sleet. The trail would be more treacherous than ever. It proved to be the worst day so far.

Often Sacagawea had seen Captain Lewis writing in his books on a little desk that was carried on a packhorse by day and taken into camp every night. On this stormy, hazardous day, the horse carrying his desk slipped and rolled downhill until a stand of scrub pine stopped his fall. Again the party was held up while the damage was assessed. When word came up to the waiting riders, it was an order to start on. The horse apparently would be able to travel. Captain Lewis's desk, however, was smashed to bits. Sacagawea felt sorry about the captain's loss, but she felt happy that the horse was not badly hurt. In the days that followed, however, one horse or two would be lost daily, either giving out from exhaustion or falling and being hurt too severely to travel.

As the first half of September slipped away, the food supply became almost nonexistent. No longer were there berries for Sacagawea to gather; neither were there edible seeds or roots. The only game on the mountains seemed to be grouse. The men were becoming discouraged and disheartened as day after day they struggled on, cold, hungry, and wondering if all their efforts were in vain. Would they ever get across the Rockies?

Sacagawea was probably the most helpful member of the party. She knew, as did Toby, that members of her race had crossed this range. It was from them that there had come stories of the Big Water, beyond.

Finally, one night when the hunting party had not even been able to find grouse, the captains decided that to get meat, they must shoot a colt that had been following its mother. Sacagawea shook her head. Her tribe had never eaten either horse or dog. Although the smell of the meat cooking over the campfire was tantalizing, when it was dished up, she would not eat. Shoshone did not eat horse meat; horses were their friends. This she asked Charbonneau to tell the captains, who were trying to insist on her eating.

Neither would she give Pomp even a taste of the juice from the meat. He would have to get along that night on mother's milk.

The travelers arrive at the mouth of the Columbia River

Chapter 13

"THE OTHER SIDE OF THE MOUNTAIN"

At long last the perilous mountain crossing was over. According to the captains' reckoning, the date was September 17, but this meant nothing to Sacagawea. She had not faltered on the difficult trail, but she was very glad that the mountain range now lay behind them. She, with the rest of the party, was exhausted and hungry.

The worst of the trip was surely over, she thought, when they came out on a wide prairie. But still there was no game. Sacagawea again went out hunting edible roots and found that the camus root was plentiful. She gathered an abundance of it, and that night the men ate heartily. But on empty stomachs and with no other food to go with the camus, it made most of them ill. Sacagawea, however, who from long experience knew better than to gorge herself after a period of starvation, was not affected.

As the expedition moved on, they came upon a large village of Nez Percé Indians. Charbonneau, with his knowledge of French, was able to explain to the others that the tribe's name meant "Pierced Noses." Sacagawea laughed at this, for indeed the men wore a ring through one side of the nose with an ornament dangling from it. Most of the ornaments were shells, which Captain Lewis said they must get by trading with Indians from the coast.

Indians who lived on the Big Water? Sacagawea wanted to know.

"Close to it," Charbonneau said.

Then they must be getting near to this unimaginably wonderful sight, Sacagawea thought. Excitement again stirred in her.

At first the Nez Percés were wary of the white men. All of their women and children ran away and hid when first the party approached. But the men stood their ground, curious about the white men and especially about the black man in the group. Sacagawea, watching their astonishment, remembered how amazed she herself had been when she first saw York.

After a little, the presence of Sacagawea and little Pomp seemed to give the women courage to return. Sacagawea smiled at them, and they crept closer, surely thinking the white men could mean no harm to Indians, when an Indian woman and child traveled with them.

From the Nez Percés the captains bought dogs for meat, again being desperate for food. But as with the horse meat, Sacagawea would not eat, insisting that she was not hungry.

As they proceeded they came to a second Nez Percé village near a river that the Indians called the Kooskooskee. The weather was now very warm, in great contrast to the chill of the mountains from which they had just come. This sudden change in temperature, together with lack of proper diet, made most of the men ill. So with plans for again taking to the rivers, they remained here a number of days both for the men to recuperate and to build canoes.

Sacagawea welcomed the time by the river, for the opportunity to bathe herself and Pomp. After bathing her papoose, she rubbed his body with bear grease. She also greased her freshly washed hair. And while she could not communicate in words with the Nez Percé Indians, she enjoyed their obvious interest in her and her papoose as they chattered among themselves, pointing to her and shaking their heads in amazement.

When the canoes were finished and the horses had been marked to be left with the Indians until the travelers' return, the supplies, the men, and Sacagawea and Pomp were loaded into the new canoes and again took up their journey by water. There were rapids again, but they only offered a little excitement, as none were impassable. Autumn was now upon them, the mornings and evenings cool, but the midday sun warm and pleasant. There were many Indians along the riverbanks and on the islands as they proceeded farther on the waters of the Snake. The river abounded in salmon, and as the Indians fished for them, so did the white men. Sacagawea welcomed the fresh salmon in their diet. The delicious aroma of the fish as she fried them made her mouth water.

At long last they reached the Columbia, the wide river that flowed directly to the sea, to the Big Water, the captains said.

One day Captain Clark, whose canoe was in advance of the others, tied up at an island where there were five houses. As he approached the dwellings, he shot a duck "on the wing" so his party could have some food other than fish.

No one came out of any of the houses so, holding out a peace pipe, he strode to the first one and lifted the mat that served as a door covering. Inside, he saw a considerable number of people, probably twenty-five or thirty, he said afterward. The men were silent, the women and children were crying and wringing their hands. Thinking to allay their fears by smoking a pipe with them, he took out his "burning glass," held it up to the sun that streamed in from the top of the unroofed hut, and lighted the pipe.

The Indians, however, seemed only to cower the more at this, so he went outside and sat on a rock, beckoning for some to follow him and smoke. They did not come.

Then the other canoes began to arrive. As soon as Captain Clark saw the one in which Sacagawea and Pomp rode, he called "Janie, come here! Show these Indians that we are not going to hurt them."

Lightly, Sacagawea stepped from the canoe and tripped up to the nearest house. The minute the Indians within saw her, they came tumbling out, no longer afraid, knowing no war party ever carried a woman and child with them. Happily Sacagawea watched as the braves willingly smoked a pipe with Clark.

With the interpreters at work, and with the help of sign language, the Indians explained that they had thought Captain Clark was not human, that when they saw the white thing (the duck he had shot) falling from the sky, they thought it was this creature who then appeared at their door. Further, they had been frightened by the sound of his gun; and, worst of all, when he used his "burning glass," they thought he was bringing down fire from heaven!

While all of this was being explained, Sacagawea was enjoying showing off her papoose to the women.

There were still dangerous rapids that had to be conquered, rapids that caused difficulties and delays. One of the canoes was overturned when it hit a rock; some of the goods it carried were lost, the rest soaked so they must be laid out to dry by the campfire that night. The air was damp and the drying process slow. Sometimes Sacagawea wondered if the Big Water really did lie somewhere before them; if the white men really knew where they were going.

She noticed that the men often spoke the word "home," and she asked Charbonneau what it meant.

When Charbonneau explained, saying he guessed they wished they were home, she was only confused. To her, wherever they traveled by day or stopped by night was home. She did not share the men's discontent.

Day by day as they traveled the Columbia, the waves became higher and higher. The water became salty and could no longer be used for drinking. Sacagawea, who had been sick only once on the whole journey, became ill.

"You're seasick, Janie," Captain Clark told her.

Another day great booming sounds assailed her ears. What was that big noise? she wanted to know.

"It's breakers—big waves breaking on the shore, waves of that Big Water you've been wanting to see."

The fog was so dense that she could see neither waves nor shore. For the first time, she wasn't so sure that her dreams of seeing the Big Water were good dreams.

Chapter 14

SUPREME SACRIFICE

The weather was still miserable when they finally pulled their canoes out of the river, and while there seemed to be water everywhere, Sacagawea still could not really see the Big Water. The fog and the rain obscured vision. But at least on land, she no longer felt sick. So Captain Clark must have been right about what was making her feel so ill.

There were lots of Indians here, several different tribes, with many who called themselves Clatsops. They seemed to be very interested in this party of whites plus one black plus two Indians. But Sacagawea knew they had seen white people before, for they were neither particularly curious, nor were they fearful. Also they cooked in beautiful shiny kettles

Charbonneau said were "brass" and "copper." These were not Indian pots.

When the captains were trying to decide whether to build winter quarters on the north side of the river, where they had landed, or to see if a place on the south side might be better, they said, "We'll put it to a vote." While Sacagawea was not given the privilege of voting, she nevertheless expressed an opinion: "Whichever side has the most wapato would be the best," she said. The wapato was a root that resembled the potato, and which she had dug at every opportunity, to add to their diet.

Although there was no wapato nearby for Sacagawea to dig, the vote was to build on the south side. Sacagawea was content with the party with whom she had shared so many hardships in the past nine months. They were all her friends, including the black man. They treated her with respect, accepting her as one of them and giving her credit for whatever she did that was helpful. She didn't care to spend time in the huts of the Clatsop, for they were dirty, and fleas lived with them thicker than bees in a hive. She thought how horrible it would be to get her own and little Pomp's clothing infested with them.

As the men felled pines and split them into logs for huts, Sacagawea cooked wapato for them as often as the captains were able to purchase it from natives who brought it from up the river. The hunters were bringing in some game, and the wapato was a welcome addition to their meals, taking the place of bread and potatoes. Furthermore, the wapato did not upset the digestive systems of the men as the camus root had. Sacagawea was doing her best to learn what available foods agreed with them and what did not.

The weather continued to be dark and dismal. Sacagawea longed to see the sun, to have it to dry out their soggy clothing and gear. But no sun came, so fires had to suffice. Every day it rained, and yet the cabins were going up.

Finally there came the day when the captains' cabin was ready to be occupied. It had been built around the stump of a big tree, and Sacagawea laughed in delight when she saw that this had been done to give the captains a table on which to write. While they were here, at least, the stump would take the place of Captain Lewis's ruined desk.

As the gloomy days wore on, many of the men became ill, and their spirits were low. Sacagawea was alarmed when even York came down with a bad cold and a fever. She was even more disturbed when Captain Clark took to his bed and refused to eat. What could she do to get him to eat, she wondered. People had to eat to live. One day when she took him a plate of elk meat and wapato and he turned his head to the wall, refusing it, she asked him what he would like. What would sound good?

"Bread," he replied. "Bread, Janie. How long since we have had bread?"

It had been months, she knew. But the moment he said, "Bread," she knew what she would do.

She ran from the room and minutes later returned, light of foot and of heart, her eyes shining. "Bread," she said, holding out to him a small piece of dry bread.

"Janie! Where on earth did you get this?" the captain asked as he took the bread from her hand.

She had saved her portion many times, to be given to Pomp when he should need it. There was more, "Eat!" she said. And he did. Sacagawea's eyes lighted up. She was very glad she had not always eaten her bread.

However, the bread was not enough to cure the redhead. So Sacagawea fixed dishes she hoped would tempt his appetite and be beneficial. The hunters had just shot several elk, the first since they had crossed the mountains. Joyously, Sacagawea set about to make elk soup for the ailing captain.

After a few days she was happy to see that he was feeling better. Perhaps the special dishes she had prepared for him had helped.

One winter's day, after Captain Clark was up and about again, a Clatsop came to the cabin to trade. He carried several furs, any one of which Sacagawea would have loved to have, but the most beautiful thing he brought was a robe made of two pure white sea-otter pelts. Almost immediately she saw that Captain Clark also thought the robe special. He wanted it. He began bargaining with the Clatsop. Out of their remaining supply of trade items, he brought forth, one by one, the things that were left: hand mirrors, medals, bright beads. But the Indian only shook his head. Usually beads were the most wanted item, and of these there were still strings of red and green and white. But there were no blue. For some reason, the blue beads had been the favorite with whatever tribe the captains had dealt.

"But we do not have any blue beads," Clark insisted.

The Indian rolled up the white fur robe, preparing to depart.

Sacagawea had been watching the whole performance, and she saw how disappointed the redhead was that he could not obtain the white robe. She had been sitting on the floor, a little distance away from where the Clatsop, Clark, and Charbonneau as interpreter, had been bargaining. Now she sprang up, and in one single motion removed her blue beaded belt that Captain Clark had given to her at Pomp's birth, and which she treasured above all other possessions, and handed it to the redheaded captain.

Clark shook his head. "Oh, no, Janie, I wouldn't want to take your belt."

But the eyes of the Clatsop grew bright with interest. He unrolled the robe, spreading it on Clark's knees.

Sacagawea dropped her belt onto the snowy white fur. The blue beads sparkled against it like the sunny sky. Clark was still shaking his head, but Sacagawea nodded hers in the affirmative, said, "Sa'i! Sa'i!" and ran from the room. It was her ultimate sacrifice. But she wanted the captain to be happy.

Chapter 15

THE BIG WATER AND THE BIG FISH

What the captains called "Fort Clatsop" was made up of seven cabins, four on one side and three on the other, with a parade ground between the two rows. By December 22, all of the cabins were finished and the men had moved in. But Sacagawea could see that even this shelter did not greatly improve the depressed spirits of the men. Many continued to be ill. They had not seen the sun in a month, and daily drizzling rain kept them inside much of the time.

Sacagawea busied herself with making moccasins and helping to mend the men's clothing and gear. Little Pomp seemed the only bright spot in the long winter days. The men played with him and made him laugh, and this made *them* laugh. He would soon be a year old.

One day two of the men who had been sent out to locate a good campsite for distilling salt came into the captains' cabin in great excitement. Sacagawea tried to follow the story they were telling. It seemed that some great beast out of the Big Water was beached on the ocean shore some thirty-five miles away. Indians who had seen it said it was monstrous. No one would believe its size unless he had seen it. The Indians had taken huge amounts of blubber from it and had given the men some. The captains said the monstrous fish must be a whale.

That evening there was talk of little else among the men. This was something to think about besides their miserable condition, something the like of which none of them had ever seen. It would be worth the thirty-five mile trek to see it. Sacagawea thought so too.

Those thirty-five miles would not be easy traveling, however, Charbonneau reported to her.

In her heart Sacagawea was excited as usual, though she didn't show it. What would it be like to see an animal as big as this cabin in which they lived? That was what the men had said of its size. And she couldn't help wondering why they should worry over a bad trail. Hadn't they followed impossibly difficult trails over the mountains? Surely this could not be as bad as that crossing had been.

All evening talk continued about the whale and about a trek to see it and to obtain blubber. The captains made plans quickly. They would take two canoes and twelve men and set out early the next morning, going by "Clatsop Town," where they hoped they would be able to pick up a guide.

No one asked Sacagawea if she would like to accompany the group to see the whale. For the first time since she had been with the expedition, she felt that she was not being treated fairly. She had come all this way to see the Big Water, and she had not yet seen it. Now there was the added pull of the great beast. She expressed her discontent to Charbonneau: "I have come all this way," she said. "I have done everything I've been told to do. I've done all I could to be helpful. I want to see the Big Water and the big fish! Tell Captain Clark what I say."

Sacagawea continued to badger Charbonneau with demands that he tell Captain Clark she wanted to go with the men to see the whale. At last, in exasperation, he told the captain of her wishes, adding, however, "She does not need to go. I am just telling you what she says because she keeps after me every minute."

"Bring Janie here," Captain Clark said.

Charbonneau found her scraping a skin, preparing it for drying. "Come!" he said to her gruffly. "The captain says 'Come,' so he can scold you. You are only a squaw. You do not need to see things."

But Captain Clark did not scold. Janie stood before him, her eyes sullen, until she saw his bright smile and heard his words, translated by Charbonneau. "Of course you can go, Janie. I had no idea you wanted to." Then her eyes brightened with joy. "But," he added, "I think it best that you leave Pomp here. The weather is so bad and the trail treacherous, they say."

"Sa'i! Sa'i!" Sacagawea said, bobbing her head up and down in delight.

The next morning the party started out. They soon found that the rigors of the trail had not been exaggerated. At one time their ascent of a steep hillside was reminiscent of their trail over the Rockies, only then their horses had to find footing; now the men and Sacagawea had this task. It didn't bother Sacagawea. She grabbed hold of a scrub pine to pull herself upward, then found a root she could put her moccasined foot on.

"She scrambles up these steep slopes like a mountain goat," Captain Clark said.

They came to the place where the men who had been sent out to get salt from the seawater had established their camp. They were being very successful, they said, already having three quarts of salt, which they proudly displayed. Curious, Sacagawea wanted to see how they did this amazing thing, but Captain Clark said they must move on.

By the time they had reached this salt camp, the roar of the breakers was pounding in their ears. The sound was as exciting to Sacagawea as it had been when she first heard it as they came up the Columbia. Then it had somehow spoken fear to her, but now it spoke brightly of an exciting dream about to come true.

The last five miles of their way, they took along the beach. The men were reluctant to stop for more than a minute when they first came into sight of the ocean, so Sacagawea, her heart pounding in excitement, had to be content with looking as she walked. The morning they had started out, the sky had been grey, as it had been all the other days at Clatsop, but now as they walked the cool, hard-packed sand of the beach, suddenly the sun came out. They stopped in their tracks, amazed and delighted. The men whooped and hollered like schoolboys out at the end of the day. But Sacagawea was very still, gazing at the great expanse of water that had suddenly gone from grey to blue. Why, she could see no end to it, any way she looked! What a world of wonders there were for one who went looking! Always, as long as she could remember, she had been curious about what lay on the other side of a hill. Now she had seen "the other side" of many a hill and mountain, and the sights she had seen filled her with awe. "Sa'i! Sa'i!" she said reverently.

But the men had started on. She ran to keep up. Surely this sun that they had not seen for so many days was a wonderful, good sign.

And then they came upon what was left of the big fish. It was little more than a skeleton now. But the size of it! The men said, "It must have been a young whale. It's not very big as whales go."

But to Sacagawea, it was big beyond belief. To think that in that great expanse of water out there, animals as big as this lived! In her mind, she was indelibly inscribing every detail of this amazing sight she was privileged to see: the length and circumference of the big fish, the vastness and the glistening beauty of the Big Water. She must store it all so that when Pomp was old enough to understand, she could describe these wonders to him.

Chapter 16

A PLACE IN HISTORY

Now that she had seen the big fish and the Big Water, Sacagawea was content. She was glad when the men began making preparations for the return journey. It had been a long winter on the damp, rainy coast with much sickness and only Pomp and Cruzatte's music to liven the dullness of the days.

It was in March that they started the long trek back. There were no plans to return by way of the Shoshone villages, so Sacagawea did not have the anticipation of seeing her people again. Still, she was her usual cheerful, helpful self on the return trip. There were again roots to dig. She acted as guide when the party reached the territory with which she was familiar from childhood. And always there was Pomp, who had had his first birthday before the expedition started homeward. Then too there was York, whom she always found entertaining, and the redheaded captain who was so kind to her.

There were some bad times on the return journey: the week when Pomp was very ill; the area where the mountain passes were filled with twelve-foot-deep snow; the times when horses were lost; the touch-and-go meeting with a band of Blackfoot Indians. But with poultices of wild onion applied to his swollen neck, Pomp recovered. Despite the snow, the mountains were finally crossed. The expedition reloaded and managed with fewer horses. The Blackfeet had not attacked. All in all the journey was easier than their first. From day to day Sacagawea knew satisfaction in the part she was playing.

So the days and the weeks went by. It was the end of June by the time the party was over the mountains. They found their canoes in good shape where they had left them. Floating down the rivers with the current during long, sunny summer hours Sacagawea found made pleasant days. One day the captains reported they had made the unheard-of distance of eighty miles.

Now the days seemed to be going too fast for Sacagawea. Once the expedition reached the Hidatsa camps, her exciting, amazing life with the Lewis and Clark excursion would be over. But before that time came, there was a day that brought joy to her heart.

They had come to a tall pillar of rock that would always be a landmark on the trail west. They stopped to examine it, exclaiming over its unique formation. Yes, it was a marvel! But to Sacagawea an even greater marvel was the fact that Captain Clark was naming it "Pomp's Tower." It was exciting that the redheaded captain was carving his name and the date, July 25, 1806, on the base of the tower, but not as exciting as having him name the landmark for her little one.

That evening Charbonneau told her that the captains had even put the name "Pomp's Tower" in their big books that they wrote in. It was something for Sacagawea to hold in her heart in the years to come: her little Pomp's name memorialized forever.

It was mid-August when the Hidatsa villages came into sight, the end of the journey for Sacagawea. For a year and four months she had played an important role in the expedition that explored and mapped the vast country of the Louisiana Purchase, considered one of the greatest journeys of exploration in the history of the United States of America. But to Sacagawea they were not history-making months; they were months of happiness—of seeing what lay on the other side of the mountains, and of satisfaction in being helpful and appreciated.

Little did she realize that her name would go down in

American history as one of the country's most important women of all time. She only knew that once they were back at the Hidatsa camp, this glorious time in her life would be ended.

On that last day, Captain Clark offered to take Pomp to St. Louis, to raise and educate him. But Sacagawea was terrified at the suggestion.

"No! No!" she cried, clutching Pomp to her breast.

"Oh, Janie," Captain Clark said, "I didn't mean to frighten you. Of course I wouldn't take Pomp from you if you don't want to let him go. It's just that he's such a fine little fellow, and I could give him advantages that you can't." He talked further to Charbonneau about his proposition, but when the two turned to Sacagawea again, she only shook her head and clutched Pomp the tighter. Charbonneau explained to Clark: "Pomp is still a baby and needs his mother. Perhaps when he is older—we will see."

The captains paid Charbonneau the five hundred dollars they had promised him for his services as an interpreter. Sacagawea received nothing. She had expected nothing. She was "only a squaw."

Sadly she watched the boats and the men go on down the Missouri without them. It twisted her heart to see them go. Perhaps she would have felt less bereft had she known that her name and appreciative words about her had gone down in the captains' big books: "This man (Charbonneau) has been very serviceable to us and his wife particularly among the Shoshones. Indeed she has borne with a patience truly admirable, the fatigues of so long a route, encumbered with the charge of an infant."

She did not know. But she was Indian. She would cope with her loss stoically. She turned to dreaming of the future, of what it might hold for Pomp, as she had dreamed of what might lie ahead for her when she had learned she was to be going on the expedition.

But it was no dream that she had become a part of history.

Sacagawea 1787?-1812

1787 Sacagawea is born. Philadelphia convention meets to frame a constitution. The constitution of the United States is signed and the U.S. government is formed. Delaware, Pennsylvania, New Jersey, and Georgia ratify the constitution and become the first four states. The Northwest Ordinance, which provides for government of the Northwest Territory, is enacted. The American inventor John Fitch launches a steamboat on the Delaware River. Dollar currency is introduced in the United States.

1788 Connecticut, Massachusetts, Maryland, New Hampshire, South Carolina, Virginia, and New York ratify the constitution. New York is declared the federal capital of the United States. The first cigar factory opens in Hamburg, Germany.

1789 The first United States Congress meets in New York. George Washington is inaugurated as president. North Carolina ratifies the constitution and becomes the twelfth state. The United States declare themselves an economic and customs union. The French Revolution begins. A Paris mob storms the Bastille. The first steam-driven cotton factory opens in Manchester, England. Chrysanthemums are introduced to Britain from the Orient.

1790 Philadelphia becomes the federal capital of the United States. The District of Columbia is founded. Rhode Island ratifies the constitution. The first Roman Catholic bishop is consecrated in America: John Carroll of Baltimore. Benjamin Franklin dies. Jews in France are granted full liberties.

1791 The first ten amendments to the United States Constitution (Bill of Rights) are ratified. Indians, armed by the British, defeat United States forces near the Wabash River in Ohio. Vermont becomes the fourteenth state. The waltz becomes fashionable in England. Samuel F.B. Morse, the inventor of the telegraph, is born. The London School of Veterinary Surgery is founded. Wolfgang Amadeus Mozart dies.

1792 Kentucky becomes the fifteenth state. The French Republic is proclaimed. Denmark is the first nation to abolish the slave trade. Two political parties are formed in the United States: the Republicans, under Thomas Jefferson, and the Federalists, under Alexander Hamilton and John Adams. Construction of the White House begins in Washington. Illuminating gas is used in England for the first time. Dollar coinage is minted in United States.

1793 The building of the Capitol begins in Washington, D.C. The Reign of Terror begins in France; King Louis XVI and Queen Marie Antoinette are executed. The Louvre becomes the national art gallery of France. Sir Alexander Mackenzie crosses the continent of Canada from coast to coast. Eli Whitney invents the cotton gin. United States law compels escaped slaves to return to their owners.

1794 The United States navy is established. "Tammany, or the Indian Chief," one of the earliest American operas, by James Jewitt, is performed in New York. Slavery is abolished in the French colonies. The Reign of Terror ends in France. The world's first technical college opens in Paris.

1795 Spain and the United States establish boundaries between Florida and the United States and navigational rights on the Mississippi River. The metric system is adopted in France.

1796 George Washington, refusing to accept a third term, delivers his Farewell Address. John Adams defeats Thomas Jefferson in the presidential election. Tennessee becomes the sixteenth state. Physician Edward Jenner introduces a vaccination against smallpox. Freedom of the press is established in France. The first horse-drawn railroad is built in England. The metric system is adopted in France.

1797 Napoleon defeats the Austrians at Rivoli and advances toward Vienna. German astronomer H.W.M. Olbers publishes his method of calculating the orbits of comets. England begins to export iron. The first copper pennies are minted in England.

1798 Income tax is introduced in England. Italian emigration to Canada begins. Ludwig van Beethoven writes his first piano concerto.

1799 George Washington dies. The Rossetta Stone is found in Egypt, making the deciphering of hieroglyphics possible. The Royal Institution is founded in Britain.

1800 United States federal offices are moved to Washington, D.C., the new capital city. Thomas Jefferson is elected president. The Library of Congress in Washington, D.C. is established. The Royal College of Surgeons is founded in London. Richard Trevithick, an English engineer and inventor, constructs a light-pressure steam engine. Letter post is introduced in Berlin, Germany.

1801 President Thomas Jefferson begins to plan an expedition that would chart a route to the Pacific Northwest. The Act of Union of Great Britain and Ireland comes into force. Robert Fulton produces the first submarine *Nautilus*. The Union Jack becomes the official flag of the United Kingdom.

1802 Napoleon becomes president of the Italian Republic. John Dalton introduces atomic theory into chemistry. Congress sets up West Point military academy in New York. The term "biology" is coined by German naturalist Gottfried Treviranus. Horse racing is introduced in England.

1803 Preparations for the exploration of the northwest with Meriwether Lewis and William Clark begin. The United States completes the Louisiana Purchase by buying a large tract of land from the Gulf of Mexico to the northwest (including Louisiana and New Orleans) from France. Ohio becomes the seventeenth state. Robert Fulton propels a boat by steam power.

1804 Lewis and Clark leave St. Louis on the beginning of their explorations. Napoleon crowns himself emperor of France. France and Britain go to war. Alexander Hamilton is killed in a duel with Aaron Burr. The first dahlias are planted in England.

1805 Sacagawea's son Jean Baptiste "Pomp" is born on February 11. Sacagawea starts off on the expedition with Lewis and Clark. The expedition crosses the Rockies in spring, reaches the Columbia River in the fall, and finally sees the Pacific Ocean. Jefferson begins his second term as president. Napoleon is crowned king of Italy. Britain and the United States break over trade with the West Indies. Rockets are introduced by Sir William Congreve as weapons into the British army. Niccolo Paganini begins to tour Europe as a violin virtuoso.

1806 Lewis and Clark complete their exploration of the northwest and return to St. Louis. Sacagawea returns to her village. British occupy the Cape of Good Hope. Napoleon enters Berlin. A scale is developed to measure wind strength.

1807 The United States establishes an embargo against Britain and France. Street lighting by gas is begun in England. England prohibits the slave trade. Robert Fulton's paddle steamer *Clermont* navigates the Hudson River.

1808 The United States prohibits the importation of slaves from Africa. The French army occupies Rome, Italy, invades Spain, and takes Barcelona and Madrid. Pigtails disappear from fashion for men's hair. Extensive excavations begin at Pompeii, Italy.

1809 James Madison becomes the fourth president of the United States. Abraham Lincoln is born. Napoleon annexes the Papal States. Louis Braille, inventor of a system of reading for the blind, is born.

1810 Napoleon is at his zenith. Venezuela, under the leadership of Simón Bolívar, breaks away from Spain. Nicolas-François Appert develops techniques for canning food. The first public billiard rooms are opened in England. The sale of tobacco is made a government monopoly. Phineas Barnum, the American showman, is born.

1811 Alexander Graham Bell writes a book on the anatomy of the brain. Venezuela and Paraguay declare their independence from Spain. Johann Meyer, a Swiss mountaineer, climbs the Jungfrau in the Alps.

1812 Sacagawea dies. Louisiana becomes the eighteenth state. The United States declares war on Britain. Napoleon enters Russia. James Madison is elected president. The steamship *Comet* operates on the Clyde River in Scotland. The Royal yacht *Squadron* is launched.

INDEX- *Page numbers in boldface type indicate illustrations.*

ABOUT THE AUTHOR

Marion Marsh Brown grew up on a farm in Nebraska, loved her life there, and attributes much of her success as an author to those early years. Now a widow, she lives in Omaha. She has one son and three grandchildren.

For a number of years she was a professor of English at the University-of-Nebraska-Omaha, but took early retirement in order to devote more time to writing. She continues, however, to teach writing classes and to lecture at writers' conferences and seminars. She is a past president of the Nebraska Writers Guild and current secretary of the Omaha Branch of the National League of American Pen Women.

Her favorite leisure-time activities are reading and traveling.

She is the author of seventeen published books, some two-thirds of them for young readers.